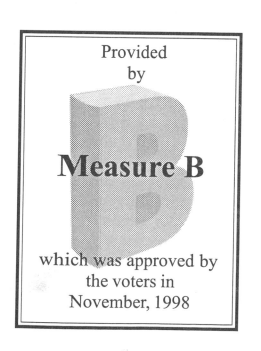

Provided
by

Measure B

which was approved by
the voters in
November, 1998

Word Bird's Fall Words

Published in the United States of America by The Child's World®, Inc.
PO Box 326
Chanhassen, MN 55317-0326
800-599-READ
www.childsworld.com

Project Manager Mary Berendes
Editor Katherine Stevenson, Ph.D.
Designer Ian Butterworth

Library of Congress Cataloging-in-Publication Data
Moncure, Jane Belk.
Word Bird's fall words / by Jane Belk Moncure.
p. cm.
Summary: Word Bird puts words about fall in his word house—
leaves, harvest, football, Pilgrims, and others.
ISBN 1-56766-895-X (lib. bdg.)
1. Vocabulary—Juvenile literature. 2. Autumn—Juvenile literature.
[1. Vocabulary. 2. Autumn.] I. Title.
PE1449 .M528 2001
428.1—dc21
00-010889

Word Bird's

Fall Words

by Jane Belk Moncure

illustrated by Chris McEwan

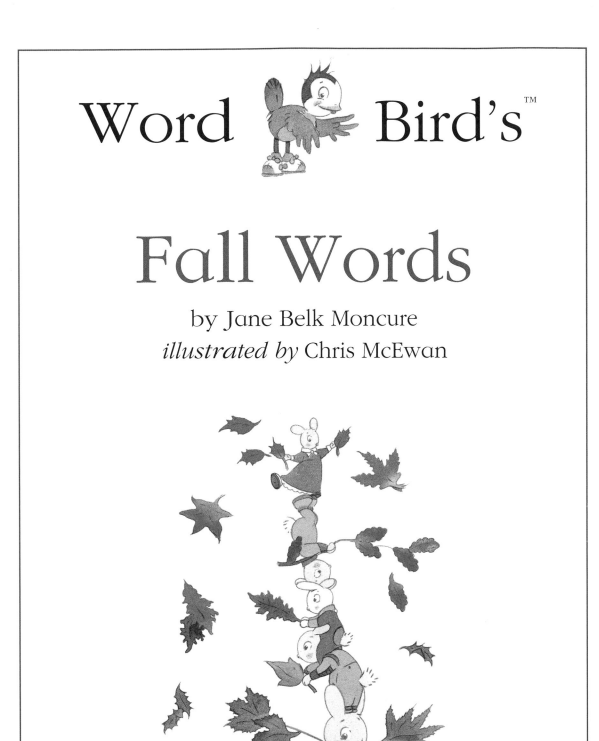

Word Bird made a…

word house.

"I will put fall words in my house," Word Bird said.

Word Bird put in
these words:

school bus

lunch box

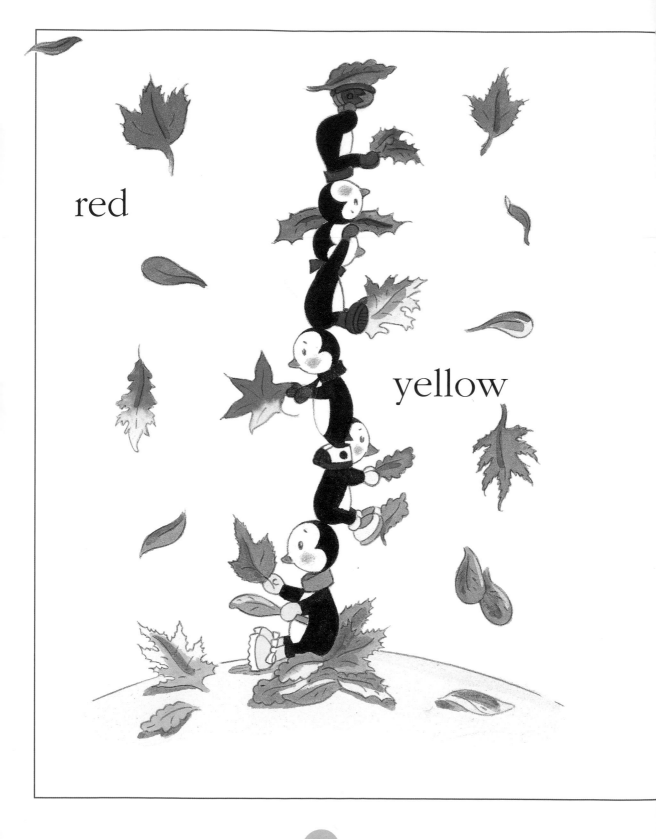

red

yellow

orange

brown

leaves

rakes

frost

football

acorns

squirrels

caterpillars

cocoons

Columbus Day

harvest

pumpkins

Halloween

jack-o'-lantern

apple cider

turkey

Pilgrims

Native Americans

Thanksgiving dinner

Can you read these fall

school bus

acorns

lunch box

squirrels

leaves

caterpillars

rakes

cocoons

frost

football

Columbus
Day

words with Word Bird?

harvest

turkey

pumpkins

Pilgrims

Halloween

Native Americans

jack-o'-lantern

apple cider

Thanksgiving dinner

You can make a fall word house. You can put Word Bird's words in your house and read them, too.

Can you think of other fall words to put in your word house?